HIDDEN WORLDS

# NATIVE AMERICANS and MESA VERDE

by Hazel Mary Martell

A ZOË BOOK

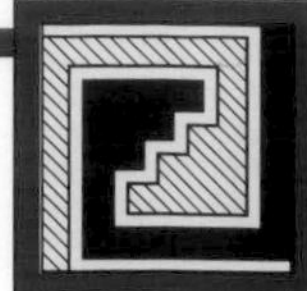

*A ZOË BOOK*



Devised and produced by
Zoë Books Limited
15 Worthy Lane
Winchester
Hampshire SO23 7AB
England



First published in Great Britain in 1993 by
Zoë Books Limited
15 Worthy Lane
Winchester
Hampshire SO23 7AB

A record of the CIP data is available from the British Library.

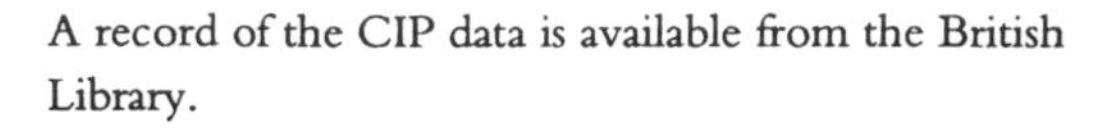

ISBN 1 874488 13 4

Printed in Italy by Grafedit SpA
Design: Jan Sterling, Sterling Associates
Picture research: Suzanne Williams
Illustrations: Shane Marsh, Cecilia Fitzsimons
Maps: Gecko Limited
Production: Grahame Griffiths

**Photographic acknowledgements**
The publishers wish to acknowledge, with thanks, the following photographic sources:

Museum of Northern Arizona, photo Marc Gaede: front cover (86C.9), 29b (86C.5); Courtesy of Mesa Verde National Park, Colorado: 7b, 8 / Gilbert Wenger, 10t & b, 11, 12t, 14t; Courtesy of Gilbert Wenger: title page, 5t, 6, 7t, 9t & b, 12b, 13, 16, 17t & b, 18, 19t & b, 20t & b, 21, 22, 23t & b, 24, 25t, 28t; Werner Forman Archive: 5b / Colorado State Museum, Denver, 25b / American Museum of Natural History, New York; Zefa: 28b.

# Contents

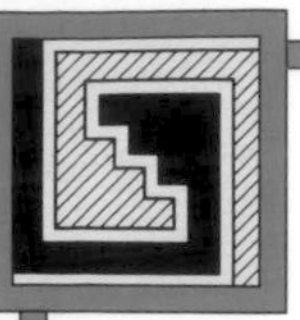

# Introduction

Native Americans is the name we give to the people who lived in America before the Europeans went there in the sixteenth century. Native Americans originally came from Asia about 40 000 years ago, when the lands now called Siberia and Alaska were linked together.

For many thousands of years, these people lived by hunting animals and gathering food. They moved around, following the animals. Their way of life is called **nomadic**.

The biggest change came about 2000 years ago. At this time corn, or **maize**, was brought north from central America to what is now southern Colorado. People realized that maize seeds could be planted, and would grow into a new crop the following season. So they began to

▶ This map shows Mesa Verde and where it is in Colorado, USA. The Anasazi people lived and farmed here for about 700 years.

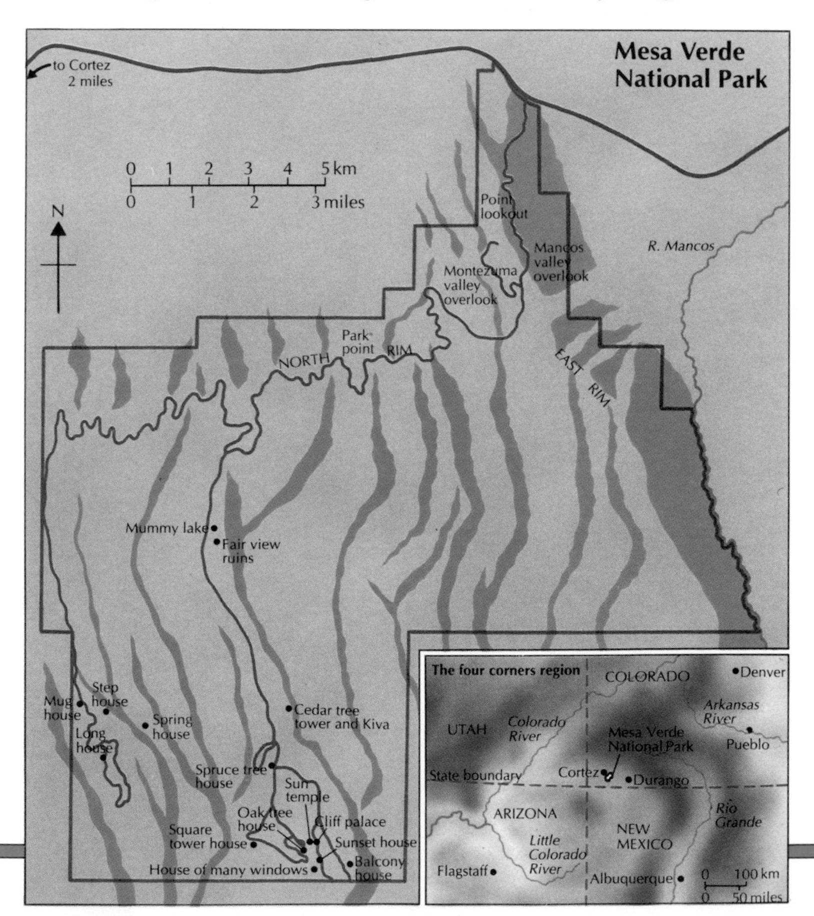


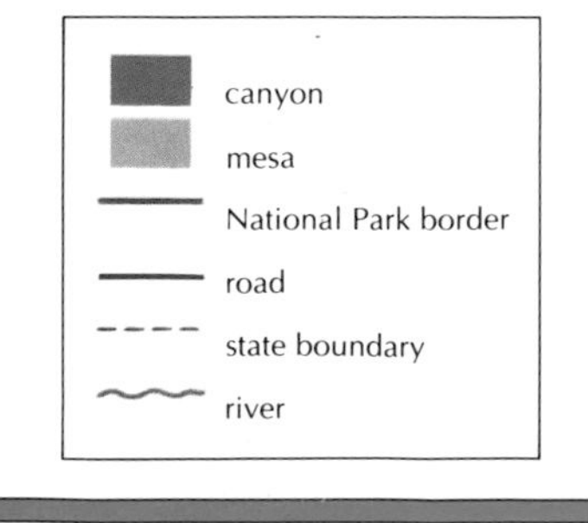

◀ The name Mesa Verde comes from the Spanish, and means 'green table'. As you can see from this photograph, the hilltops are flat, but the sides are very steep. The highest point is 2617 metres above sea level. Although the climate was dry, there was plenty of wood for building and for fires. There was also fertile soil on the **mesa** tops, where wild fruits and nuts grew, to add variety to the diet.

grow their own food. They were farmers.

These were the earliest of the **Anasazi**, or Ancient Ones. They are often known as 'Basketmakers' because they used baskets instead of pottery to cook in and eat from. They settled around Mesa Verde, but there is no trace of them in Mesa Verde itself until about AD 550. By this time they were living in **pithouses**, making their first crude pottery and growing corn and **squash** to eat. Over the next 700 years their culture developed, until by AD 1250 they were living in stone buildings up to four storeys high. These buildings were like apartment blocks and are now known as **pueblos**. Although the Anasazi had no wheeled vehicles or horses, they traded goods over a wide area. They worked out ways of irrigating their crops in the dry or **semi-arid** climate.

Then, in 1273, the Anasazi began to leave Mesa Verde and never went back. They left no written records of what their lives were like, but they did leave many clues in the form of the things they made, their **artefacts**, and buildings. People who study these remains are called **archaeologists**. They have gradually built up a picture of what life was like in Mesa Verde from AD 550 to AD 1300.

▼ The early Anasazi used baskets like this one for carrying things. The patterns were often painted on, rather than woven into the basket.

# The history of Mesa Verde

The Basketmakers probably discovered the Mesa Verde area by chance when they were out hunting and, realizing it had a water supply and fertile soil for growing crops, decided to settle there. At first the pithouses they lived in were partly below ground, but by AD 750 the people of Mesa Verde were building their houses above ground. They had flat roofs and were built in long rows, usually facing south. Behind the houses there were smaller rooms for storage. Often a pithouse was also built in front of the village, and the men used this as a meeting place.

**The Classic Pueblo Period**

Around AD 1100 the Anasazi began to build the **cliff dwellings** for which Mesa Verde is most famous. Farming, pottery, the building of water systems, and trading were all important activities. It must have taken a great deal of effort to build

▶ Archaeologists have reconstructed this pithouse in Mesa Verde National Park from evidence found in excavations. Access was through a hole in the roof, which also let out the smoke from the fire. The walls were made of wooden poles, laced together with sticks and mud. The inside walls and the floor were plastered with clay to make them smooth.

◀ Square Tower House is the tallest structure in the National Park. It dates from the Classic Pueblo Period, between AD 1100 and 1300. Originally the house had 80 rooms. Of these, 60 rooms and 7 kivas remain. The tower itself is 26 metres high.

pueblos such as Spruce Tree House with its 114 rooms and 8 **kivas**, or Long House with 150 rooms and 21 kivas. Yet by AD 1300 the area was abandoned. A **drought** which began around 1273 caused the crops to fail and, faced with starvation, the people began to move away. They headed south into New Mexico and Arizona, where both the **Acoma** and **Hopi** peoples now claim to be descended from them.

**Mesa Verde National Park**

The Anasazi never returned to Mesa Verde. Everything they had left behind remained untouched until about 90 years ago, when Cliff Palace was discovered. People began to realize how important the area was, and a campaign was started to make it a **National Park**. This was achieved in 1906 and scientific **excavation** of the area began. Mesa Verde was chosen as a World Heritage Cultural Site in September 1978.

▼ In 1917 this collection of artefacts became Mesa Verde's first museum. Standing beside it is Dr Jesse Fewkes, the first archaeologist to work at Mesa Verde. He excavated Spruce Tree House in 1908 and Cliff Palace in 1909.

# Why choose this site?

▶ This is one of the many photographs of Mesa Verde taken in 1891 by Gustaf Nordenskiold from Sweden. The pueblos were built from stone, so some of their walls were still standing and were several metres high.

The Anasazi had no horses or wheeled vehicles on which to transport heavy loads. When they abandoned Mesa Verde almost everything they used was left behind. No one moved into the area for nearly 600 years, so it remained untouched, except by the weather. As the climate is semi-arid, a lot of evidence of the Anasazi way of life was preserved.

In 1848 the Mesa Verde area became part of the USA and the land was made available for settlers. The first people to move in to the area were miners who had heard **legends** about a city built on seven hills of gold. In 1874 the first photographs were taken of an Anasazi house. The miners were followed by cattle-ranchers, and in 1881 the buildings now called Cliff Palace were discovered by two men who were looking for their cattle in a snowstorm. More ruins were found, together with many artefacts, and people started coming into the area to see what else they could find. Their favourite souvenirs were pots, so they became known as pot-hunters.

Soon people realized that the pot-hunters' activities would destroy all the evidence of the Anasazi way of life. In 1906 the area was turned into a National Park so that the ruins and the artefacts could be protected from the pot-hunters and studied by archaeologists and other experts.

**Studying in the Mesa Verde**

Since 1906, the buildings and the area have been examined by archaeologists, scientists and surveyors. These experts have worked with the staff of the National Park to excavate and preserve the artefacts and the buildings. The way the Anasazi lived has been studied by **anthropologists**. They try to work out how people lived from what they left behind. The Hopi people have also worked at Mesa Verde to find out more about their **ancestors**.

▲ This collection of artefacts was photographed at Mesa Verde about 1904. By that time, the removal of artefacts by visitors had become a serious problem.

◀ A view of the Balcony House ruin

# Excavation and recording

▲ Archaeologists today have a great deal of equipment to help them to recover information from each site. A photograph of a site taken from a high point, shows how buildings or artefacts relate to each other.

Archaeologists have been excavating and surveying at Mesa Verde for almost ninety years. In this time they have recorded almost 4000 sites relating to the Anasazi. As well as the cliff dwellings, these sites also include pithouses, work areas, water supply systems and places where fires have been lit. There are so many sites that only the most important ones have been excavated. The others have been marked and their position has been recorded on a map.

**The early years**

The archaeologists excavated Spruce Tree House in 1908 and Cliff Palace in 1909. Some of the roofs and walls had collapsed into the pueblos. This meant that as well as looking for artefacts amongst the ruins, they also had to clear out many tonnes of stone and other **debris**. They then had to repair the remaining walls to preserve them from further damage and to make them safe for visitors.

▶ Many sites at Mesa Verde are covered with a deep layer of wind-blown soil. This has to be removed with picks, shovels and wheelbarrows. Then more delicate tools have to be used. A fine brush is used to remove the soil from this skeleton.

## Later excavations

By the 1920s, the main ruins had been excavated and made safe. Many artefacts were preserved for display in a museum at Mesa Verde. By the 1950s, however, archaeology had become much more scientific, and access to Mesa Verde was much easier. Between 1958 and 1962 the National Geographic Society and the National Parks Service carried out a huge project. They gathered information, or **data**, on all aspects of the Anasazi and their environment. At the same time, the University of Colorado started a twenty-year project of surveying and excavating in Mesa Verde. They discovered many new sites. Each site is recorded in photographs and field notes, as well as on a map, so that a full report about it can be published.

▼ When the ruin of Far View House was excavated around 1920, some of the debris was removed with the help of a horse-drawn plough. Today helicopters take National Park staff and equipment to the most remote sites.

# Analysis and conservation

▲ Archaeologists study the many different shapes, designs and colours of Anasazi pottery to help them find out when and where it was made.

Some artefacts survive because the soil is waterlogged and no air can get to them. However, at Mesa Verde artefacts survived because the site was so dry. The insects and fungi which often cause rotting could not live there. Artefacts made from wood and plant fibres were found, as well as objects made of pottery and stone. All the artefacts were numbered on site. It was possible to see how one artefact related to another after they had been removed from the ground. Then the artefacts were taken to laboratories to be analysed and **conserved**, or made ready for showing to the public.

## Skeletons and mummies

The semi-arid climate at Mesa Verde meant that some bodies had not rotted away. They had dried out, or **mummified**. By studying these remains carefully, archaeologists know what the Anasazi looked like. From the size of the skeletons, they

▶ Not all artefacts are put on display to the public. Many are kept for use in research projects by archaeologists, scholars, museum staff and scientists.

◀ Artefacts made from bone, wood and plant fibres need to be stored very carefully. If they get too hot or too cold they will soon rot. Damp, fungus and insects can also damage them. To keep them safe for future researchers, they are kept in insect-proof storage cases at a regular temperature.

think that the men were about 160 centimetres tall, and the women were usually shorter. They were mostly of slight build, and very few lived beyond the age of forty. They all had dark hair. Men wore their hair long, but women often cut their hair short.

**Flattened skulls**

In their studies of skeletons from Mesa Verde, archaeologists have found that those from before about AD 750 have differently shaped skulls than more recent ones. At first they thought the original inhabitants had been replaced by a different people. Now they know that the different skull shapes were caused by the cradles people slept in as babies. In the earlier period, babies slept in soft cradles with a padded cushion for their heads, which grew to the normal shape. In later times, however, babies were strapped to hard cradle-boards. When the soft bones of their skulls hardened, they became flat at the back. Although this made their heads a different shape, it did not damage their brains.

# Environmental archaeology

▲ Archaeologists at Mesa Verde use a technique called tree-ring dating to find out how old trees are. They know that all trees of the same type put on the same thickness of growth ring each year, according to what the weather is like. In a dry or cold summer, the ring will be narrow, but in a wet summer it will be much broader. Starting with a section of a tree trunk of known age, they then try to match its tree ring pattern to that on a section of another tree trunk. They are able to tell almost exactly when a piece of timber was cut. They can also tell which were the dry summers and which were wet.

While some archaeologists study large buildings and artefacts from the past, others analyse tiny objects. Seeds, **pollen** grains, bones and insect remains are often found in the soil at an excavation. By identifying these, archaeologists can find out what a site was like at the time it was occupied. These specialists are called environmental archaeologists.

**The environment of Mesa Verde**

When the Anasazi lived in Mesa Verde, the environment was not very different from today. Trees such as piñon pines and Utah junipers grew on the mesa tops and on the slopes of the canyons. Although these trees rarely grew above 10 metres high, they provided the Anasazi with firewood, and wood for building and making tools. Nuts from the piñon pines were eaten, while the juniper berries were used for medicine and for flavouring foods. Animals in Mesa Verde included mule deer, bighorn sheep, elk, coyotes, badgers, foxes, squirrels, chipmunks and **cougars**. There were also porcupines and rabbits. The birds included turkeys, eagles, owls, ravens and **vultures**. There were also lizards, rattlesnakes and spiders called **tarantulas**.

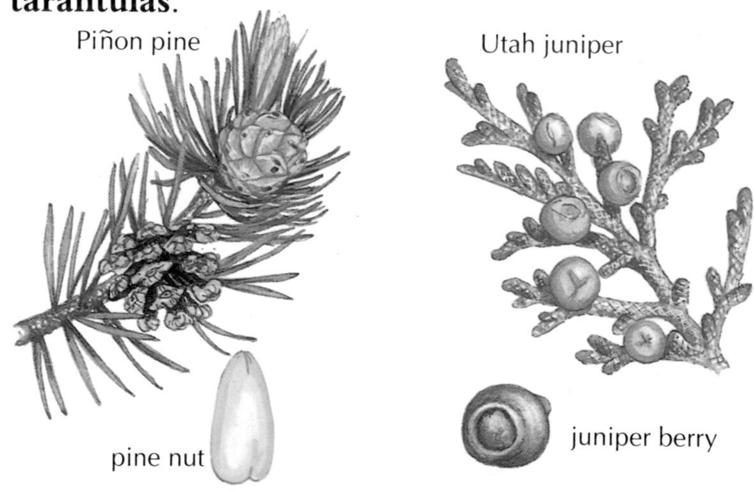

## Health and disease

One of the Anasazi's biggest problems was having enough to eat. If there were a long drought, their crops would fail and they would soon starve, or suffer from **malnutrition**. This happened just before Mesa Verde was abandoned, as skeletons from this period show that women were dying between 20 and 25 years of age, while men lived to between 31 and 35 years. Most skeletons also show signs of **arthritis** and some have fractured bones. The fractures were probably caused by falling on the steep slopes around their homes.

# At home in Mesa Verde

▲ The ruins of Cliff Palace were first excavated in 1909. The oldest part is at the back, nearest the overhanging cliff. Archaeologists believe that building started here in about 1066. Cliff Palace was abandoned during the drought which lasted from 1274 to 1299.

Most of the people of Mesa Verde lived together in communal houses or pueblos. These were two, three or four storeys high. They were often built in steps so that the flat roof of one storey could be used by the people on the next storey. The ground floor rooms had no doors or windows. To get into them, people had to climb up a ladder on the outside and drop through a hole in the roof.

The largest of these pueblos is now known as Cliff Palace. This is because it was built under the shelter of an overhanging cliff. In some ways it was like a modern apartment block, as each family had its own rooms. The rooms were about 3 metres long and 6 metres wide. The climate was warm and dry, so much work, such as preparing food and cooking it, could be done outside. The rooms were used to sleep in, and had no furniture.

Cliff Palace was built of bricks of sandstone, held together with a **mortar** of thick mud. The people who lived there had no metal and all their tools were made from stone, wood or bone. To make a fire, they twisted a hard stick in a piece of softer wood until it made a spark.

▲ The people of Mesa Verde made pottery like this around the year 1100. It was painted white and the pattern was painted on in black. As well as bowls, mugs and jars, the Anasazi also made pottery plates, jugs and ladles.

◀ Rooms on the upper floors of the pueblos at Mesa Verde had T-shaped doorways. These were set quite high in the wall and had a deep step at either side. Climbing over it would be difficult for some people, as evidence from skeletons shows that many suffered from arthritis.

# Food and farming

Although Mesa Verde had a semi-arid climate, the Anasazi were able to farm there. Most of the mesa tops were covered in a layer of fertile soil, called **loess**, and the Anasazi grew their crops in this. First, however, they had to clear the trees and bushes. They cut them down with stone axes and used the wood for building or for their fires. They also had to find ways to stop their crops from drying up when there was not enough rain. They built reservoirs to hold water, which could be carried to the crops when necessary. They also built **check dams**. These soon filled with mud or **silt** which stayed moist long enough each year for seeds to grow in it.

▼ The remains of this reservoir can still be seen at Mesa Verde. It supplied water for the people who lived in Far View House.

◀ Maize, beans and squash were the main crops grown at Mesa Verde. Samples of these crops were found in the ruins.

## Crops

The first crop to be grown at Mesa Verde was maize, or corn. This was followed by beans and squash. The Anasazi used a wooden digging stick to make a hole in the ground, then dropped the seed into it. Once the seeds began to grow, stone hoes were used to dig out any weeds which grew in between the plants. Everyone was kept busy chasing birds and animals away.

## Hunting and gathering

The people of Mesa Verde had to hunt if they wanted to eat meat. The Basketmakers used a spear, which they threw with the help of an **atlatl**. Later hunters used bows, and arrows tipped with stone points and they also made snares from **yucca** fibres. They hunted deer, mountain sheep and rabbits. After the animals had been killed, they were skinned and cut up or butchered with knives made from **obsidian** or other hard stone. The meat was either stewed or roasted and eaten with bread which had been baked on stone **griddles** over a fire. Seeds, nuts and berries were also collected from wild plants in Mesa Verde to add variety to the daily diet.

▼ The Anasazi domesticated the wild turkeys which were found at Mesa Verde. They did not seem to have kept the turkeys for food, however, as some buried turkeys have been found. Archaeologists think that the turkeys were kept as pets. They were also kept for their feathers, which the Anasazi used to make capes for the winter.

# Crafts

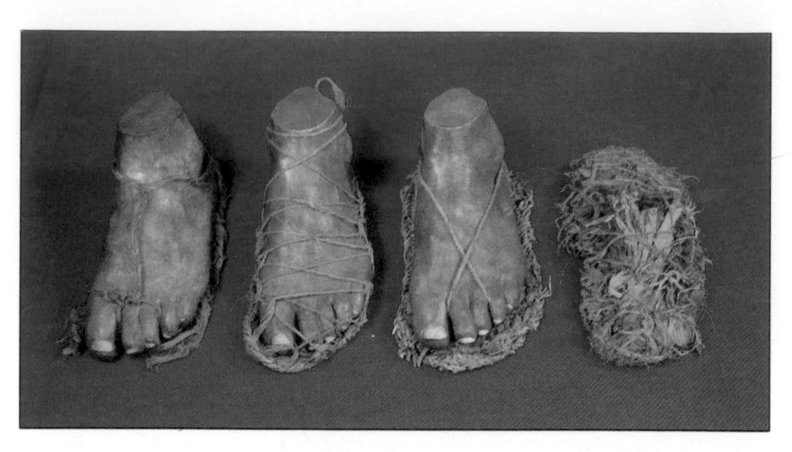

▶ Many sandals have been found at Mesa Verde. These were necessary because of the harsh environment, where many plants had thorns and the ground was covered with sharp rocks.

The earliest inhabitants of Mesa Verde cooked and ate their meals out of baskets, and used them for storing and carrying things. The baskets were usually made from willow twigs which were split to make them bend easily. A tight coil was made. This spiralled outwards and each additional coil was sewn to the previous one with a thinner length of twig. Some baskets were so tightly woven that they could be used to carry water. Others were shaped like shallow trays and were used for cooking seeds by parching. In this

▶ Mesa Verde pottery reached its peak from AD 1100 to AD 1300 in the Classic Pueblo Period. The clay usually turned a greyish-white colour when it had been baked. Geometric designs were then painted on it in black, using brushes made from the yucca plant.

method, hot **embers** were put into the basket with the seeds and shaken about until the seeds were cooked. Liquids were also cooked in baskets by dropping hot stones in them.

By about 1200 years ago, during the Pueblo Period, baskets were mainly used for carrying and storing as the Anasazi had discovered how to make pottery. Although they had no potter's wheel, they were able to shape mugs, plates, ladles and jars from the local clay.

## Clothing

Apart from sandals made from plaited yucca fibres, not much evidence of clothing has been found at Mesa Verde. This suggests that the Anasazi probably wore very little for most of the year, because the climate was usually warm and dry. When the weather turned cold, however, they wore capes made from woven yucca fibres which had been wrapped with turkey feathers or strips of rabbit skin.

## Jewellery

The Anasazi had no metals, so they made most of their jewellery from stones, bones and shells. The **turquoise** stone was popular for necklaces, and they also used **jet**, which was black, and a red stone called argillite. The Anasazi probably also had hair ornaments, rather like tall combs, made from wood, and earrings made from small bunches of feathers.

## Tools

The Anasazi used tools made from wood, stone or bone. They made axes and scrapers, knives and needles, arrowheads, drills and **awls**. These simple tools were used for everything, from cutting and shaping stone building blocks, to making looms for weaving. The men wove blankets and sleeping mats on the looms.

▼ The bone scraper on the right was used to remove meat from animal skins or hides. The Anasazi used the pointed bone drills to make holes of different sizes.

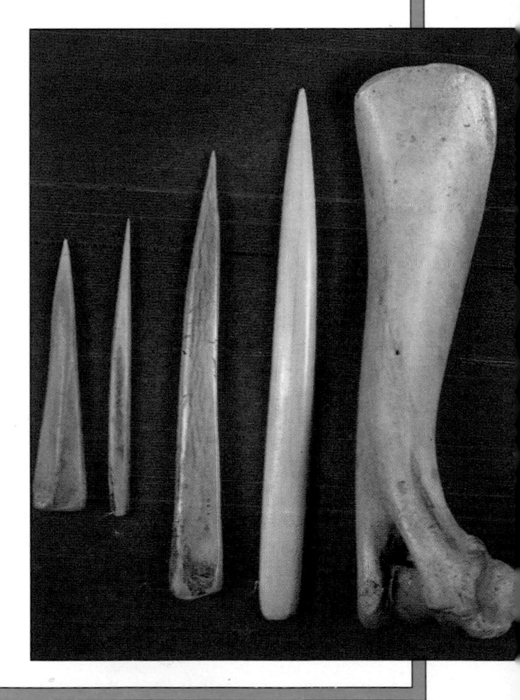

# Religion and men's work

Archaeologists at Mesa Verde have found out about religion there from the Hopi people. The Hopi claim to be directly descended from the Anasazi and to carry on many of their traditions. The Anasazi religion had close ties with nature and the environment. Spirits were thought to live in the sun, the wind, the rain and other natural elements. The Anasazi relied on the spirits to give them a good harvest, and part of the men's work may have been to plan special ceremonies to bring rain and to keep the spirits happy. Like many Hopi ceremonies today, these probably

▼ This kiva has been excavated at Mesa Verde. Originally it would have been roofed over. Fresh air came in through the ventilator shaft. To stop the wind from blowing the fire out, a stone slab, or **deflector**, was put in front of the hole where the fresh air entered the kiva.

involved some sort of dancing by the men, who perhaps painted their bodies and wore feathers in their hair for the occasion.

## Kivas

Each pueblo at Mesa Verde had one or more kivas. These were usually circular buildings which were partly below ground level. The Anasazi thought they had arrived on earth from the Four Worlds, which were just below the earth's surface. To allow spirits to come from the Four Worlds into the kiva, there was a hole called a **sipapu** in the floor of each one. The kivas were mainly meeting places for the men, although sometimes women were allowed to go in. Kivas were used for religious purposes and also for social gatherings, especially in the winter.

## Other work

As well as organizing the religious ceremonies, the men made all the tools and did most of the building. They also tended the crops in the fields on top of the mesas, and they went hunting, usually with bows and arrows. From some kivas there is evidence that they wove cotton cloth on upright looms. Some men probably also went on long journeys to trade.

▲ The Anasazi made their axe-heads from a hard rock such as granite. The rock was shaped and polished by rubbing it against another rock. A groove was then ground into the axe-head so that it could be fixed on to a wooden handle.

◀ A few paintings survive in Mesa Verde today. Some, such as these, are carved into the rock surface and are known as petroglyphs. Others, called pictographs, are painted on walls inside buildings.

# Society and women's work

Present-day Hopi people have also been able to tell archaeologists at Mesa Verde about Anasazi society, based on the way their own is organized. The Hopi live in groups or **clans** of people who are related by having the same female ancestor. In their society, the house belongs to the woman. When a daughter marries, she usually takes her husband to live in the same house as her mother, or builds another room onto her mother's house. The daughters all still belong to the same clan and so do their children. However, each husband belongs to the same clan as his own mother and sisters and their children. This type of society is called a **matriarchy**.

▼ The grains of corn, or maize, were put on the **metate** and then rubbed with the **mano** until they were ground into flour. Sometimes small pieces of the stone broke off and were ground in as well. Archaeologists know this because the teeth on most of the skeletons they have found were worn down.

◀ The women used pots like this one for cooking. They were made by shaping the clay into long rolls, then coiling them on top of each other. The coils were then pinched together on the outside to give this corrugated appearance.

▼ This apron is made from yucca fibres, woven together at the top. The apron dates from the time of the Basketmakers, more than 1200 years ago.

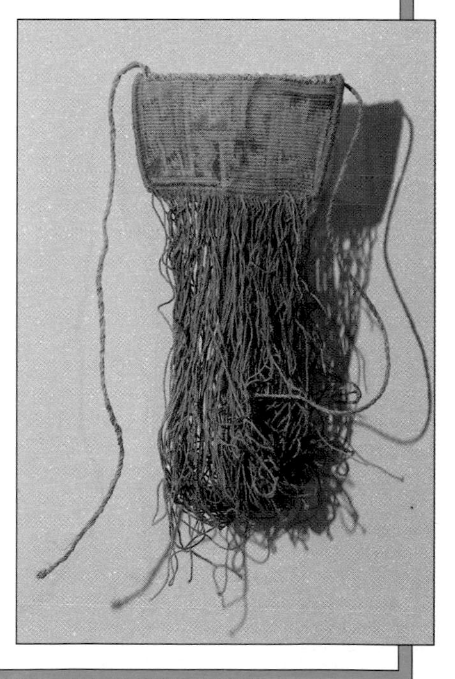

## Everyday work

Anasazi women were responsible for looking after the children. They also spent a lot of time each day grinding maize grains into flour. They used a stone mano and a metate. It was a very slow and boring job, so some pueblos had special **mealing rooms** where several women could work together and talk or sing as they worked. The women also gathered nuts, fruits and berries and did all the cooking. In summer this was done out of doors on the flat roofs and the courtyards of the pueblo, but in winter the cooking was often done inside, so that the fire also warmed the room. The women's other main task was making and decorating pottery. They also made the turkey feather cloaks for the winter and helped the men with the farming and building.

# Mesa Verde reconstructed

In summer the pueblo dwellings at Mesa Verde were busy places. Women talked or sang as they ground grain and nuts on their metates, while others tended the fires ready for cooking. They probably also made their pottery outside, and painted it where the natural light was strong enough for them to see to make their intricate patterns. The children played or slept in the sun, on the roofs of the buildings, while the dogs and the tame turkeys scavenged for food or chased each other around.

If the men were not busy in the fields, there would be plenty of work for them to do around the pueblo. They had to keep the buildings in good repair and add new rooms on to them. They probably also made and mended tools in the courtyards, shaping axes and chipping arrowheads, polishing knife-blades and putting wooden handles on them.

▼ The Anasazi did most of their work and their cooking outside. The overhanging cliffs protected them from the hot sun in the summer and the worst of the snow in the winter.

**Health hazards**

Although the Anasazi spent a lot of time outside, the air they breathed was not always good for them. Rubbish was dumped in front of the village and left to rot. If someone died in the winter, when the ground was too hard to dig a grave, the body might be buried in the rubbish. Some bodies were also placed in empty rooms near the back of the pueblo, while other empty rooms were used as toilets in the winter.

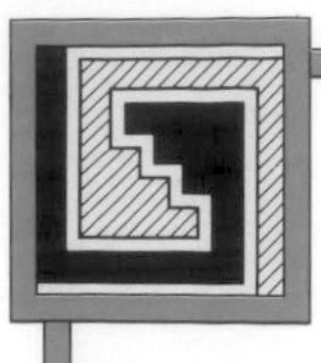

# Mesa Verde's place in prehistoric America

▲ Part of the ruins at Hovenweep National Monument. Between 400 and 500 people lived in the village which was built around this square tower. This site had been inhabited since at least AD 1, but was abandoned by AD 1300.

Ruins of Anasazi settlements can be found throughout the Four Corners area, where the states of Colorado, Utah, Arizona and New Mexico now meet. In all these places the people managed to farm the semi-arid land by making dams and watercourses to provide water for their crops. They built pithouses and then pueblos with kivas. They made baskets and later they made pottery. They all buried their dead in the same way, with their knees bent up towards their chests.

All the Anasazi communities tried to be self-sufficient, but the communities also traded with each other. Different areas used different patterns and even different shapes for their pottery, and so archaeologists can tell where any particular piece originally came from.

The Anasazi also had trading links with people

▶ Scarlet macaws were highly valued by the Anasazi. They were brought from tropical Central America. The Anasazi kept them for their feathers.

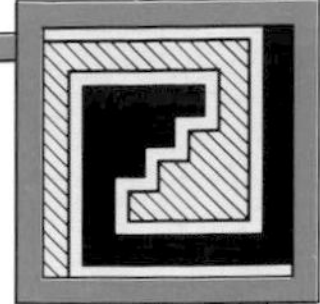

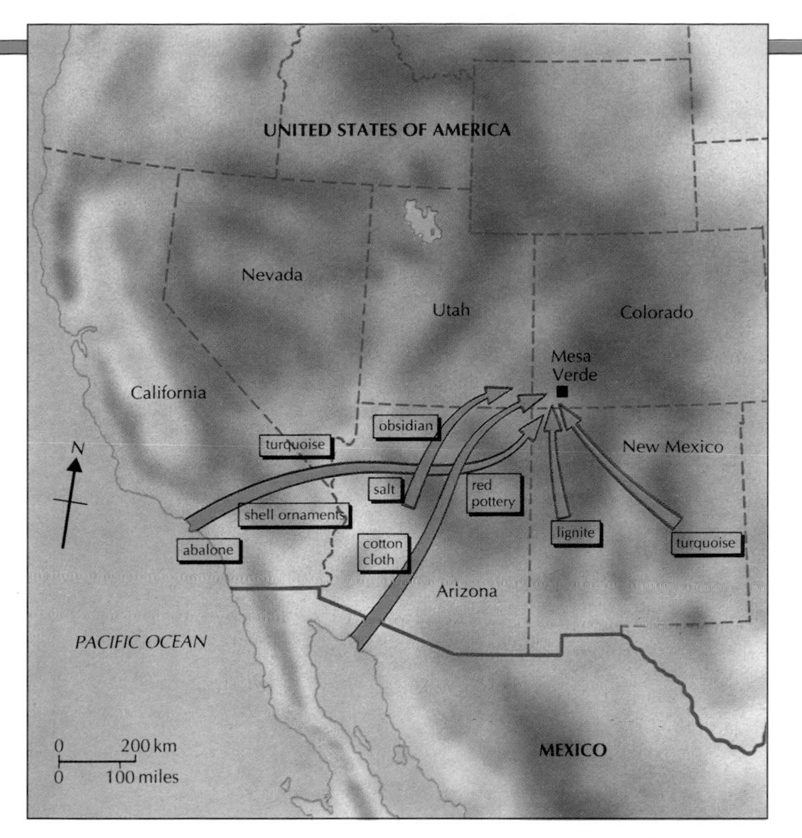


◀ This map shows some of the goods which were brought into the Mesa Verde area.

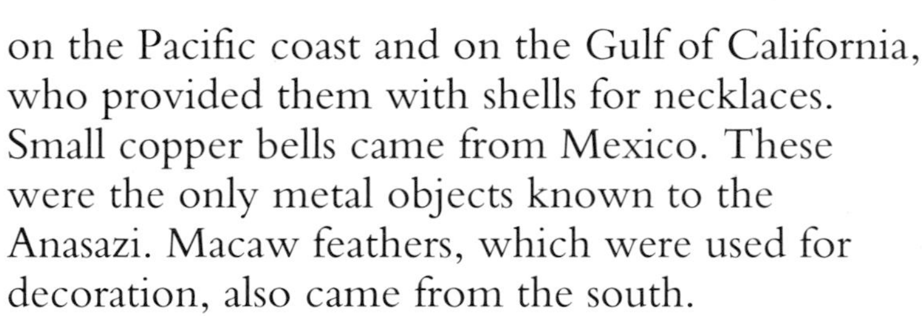

on the Pacific coast and on the Gulf of California, who provided them with shells for necklaces. Small copper bells came from Mexico. These were the only metal objects known to the Anasazi. Macaw feathers, which were used for decoration, also came from the south.

By AD 1300 the Anasazi had left the Four Corners area and moved south into the valleys of the Rio Grande and the Little Colorado rivers. The Anasazi took their pottery and their building skills with them and set up new pueblos. From 1540 onwards, however, various peoples from other countries tried to change the Anasazi way of life. First the Spaniards, then the Mexicans and finally the settlers from Europe took over their lands. Many Native Americans were killed in battles for the land. Many more died from diseases which were brought to America by the Europeans. In spite of this, some pueblos survived and are still lived in today.

▼ Present day pueblos are very similar to those in which the Anasazi lived. This one is at Taos in New Mexico.

# Glossary

**Acoma:** Native Americans who claim direct descent from the Anasazi of Mesa Verde.

**Anasazi:** Navajo word which means 'The Ancient Ones' or ancestors.

**ancestors:** people from whom someone is directly descended. For example, a grandmother or great-grandfather.

**anthropologist:** someone who makes a scientific study of people, their origins, beliefs and relationships.

**archaeologist:** someone who makes a scientific study of the past by looking for and analysing artefacts and other objects.

**arthritis:** a painful disease of the joints.

**artefact:** an object made and used by people in the past.

**atlatl:** a special stick which made it possible to throw a spear further.

**awl:** a pointed tool which is used to make holes in wood.

**check dam:** a barrier used to slow down or check water from running off small areas of farm land. The mud which built up behind the barrier helped to keep the soil damp and warm so that the seeds planted in it could grow well.

**clan:** a group of people who are related to each other.

**cliff dwelling:** an Anasazi home built under the shelter of an overhanging cliff.

**conserve:** to prepare or restore an artefact so that it stays in good condition.

**cougar:** a big American cat, also called a puma or a mountain lion.

**data:** information, often based upon observations and measurement.

**debris:** a mixture of stones and soil in buildings which are ruined.

**deflector:** a barrier set up in a kiva to make the air flow change its direction.

**drought:** an unusually long period without rain or snow.

**embers:** the glowing pieces of wood left in a dying fire.

**excavation:** the place where archaeologists dig for evidence of the past.

**griddle:** a flat, heated stone on which food can be cooked.

**Hopi:** Native Americans who claim direct descent from the Anasazi of Mesa Verde.

**jet:** a shiny black rock, like coal.

**kiva:** a building which was partly underground and was used mainly by the men for religious purposes.

**legend:** an old story which many people believe, even though it may not be quite true.

**loess:** a fine, light-coloured soil which has been carried by the wind from one place and deposited at another.

**maize:** a sort of corn which is also known as sweet corn.

**malnutrition:** the effect of either not eating enough food or not eating the right kind of food.

**mano:** the stone which was used to grind the grain into flour.

**matriarchy:** a society in which people trace their lines of descent through their mothers.

**mealing room:** a special room in a pueblo where several women could work together, grinding corn.

**mesa:** a flat-topped hill with steep sides.

**metate:** the stone on which grain was placed to be ground into flour.

**mortar:** a very thick mud which was used to hold stones together in the walls of buildings.

**mummified:** a body which has been preserved by drying.

**National Park:** an area of great natural, archaeological or historical interest which is financed and protected by the US Government.

**nomadic:** without a settled home.

**obsidian:** a dark, glassy rock from the lava of a volcano.

**pithouses:** houses which were built partly underground by the Basketmakers.

**pollen:** a yellow dust produced by flowers that fertilizes seeds.

**pueblo:** a multi-storeyed building, usually made from stone, in which several related families live.

**semi-arid:** a climate which has only a small amount of rainfall.

**silt:** a layer of fine soil which has been carried by water from one place and deposited at another.

**sipapu:** a hole in the ground through which, the Anasazi believed, spirits reach this world from one beneath.

**squash:** a fleshy vegetable similar to a pumpkin.

**tarantula:** a large spider whose bite is poisonous.

**turquoise:** a blue-green stone which is used for making jewellery.

**vulture:** a large bird of prey which feeds on bodies of dead animals.

**yucca:** a plant with stiff, pointed leaves and spikes of white flowers.

# Index